REYNOLDS' READING BOOKS VOL. 1

TONY

GETS A JOB AS A HANDYMAN

WRITTEN BY

TRON REYNOLDS

ILLUSTRATED BY

BENJAMIN OGAH

ISBN: 978-0-578-35566-5
Publishing and Design Services: Melindal

Hello there! I'm Tony,
and today I start my new job
as a handyman.
I can't wait to get started.

A job is when someone pays you money in exchange for your work.

A handyman is a person
that makes small repairs.

I use the calendar on my phone
to stay organized.
I have an appointment at 10 a.m.
to paint a wall for Mr. Hill.

Before I head to work,
I need to get dressed for
the type of work I will be doing.

Today I will be wearing
a pair of blue overalls and
brown steel toe boots.

Mr. Hill has already bought the paint, but I need to bring the rest of the supplies for painting.

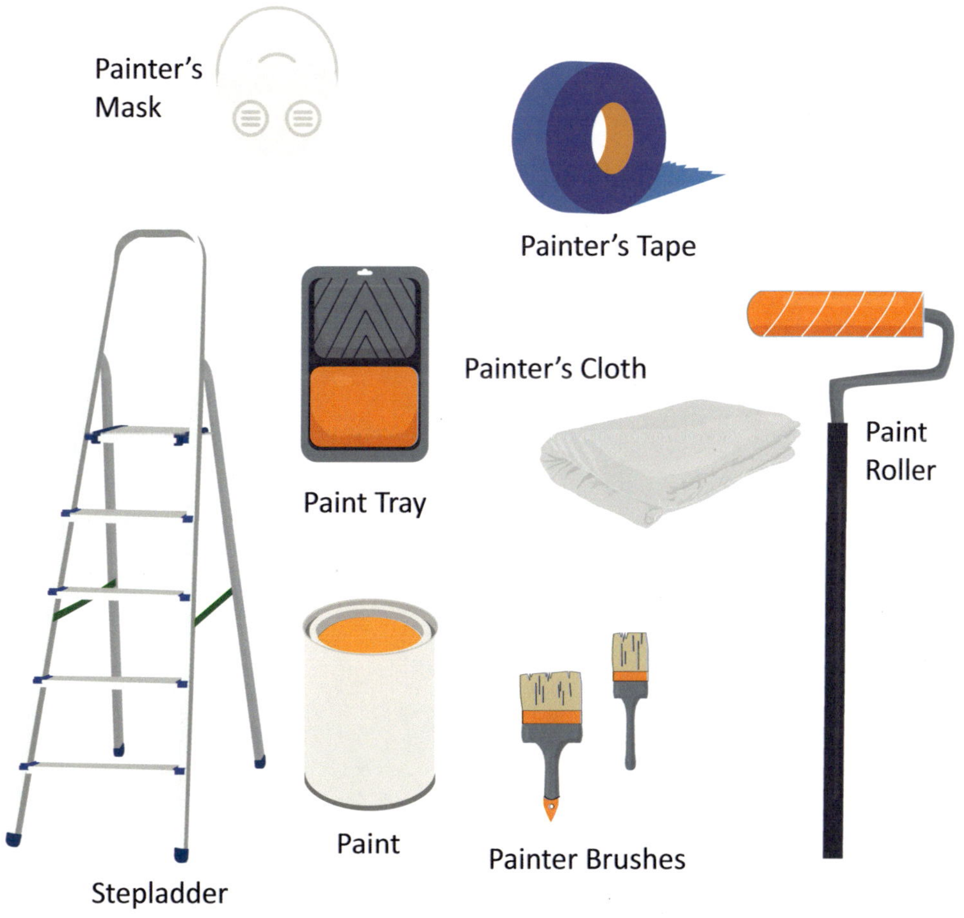

Sometimes, the customer needs to change the day or time I arrive. Before I leave, I call Mr. Hill and confirm our appointment.

If I am unable to make it on time,
I call the customer right away
to let them know.

I always try my best
to make it to work on time.
Customers plan their day around the
time I said I would be there.
It's important to keep my word.

I stop by my favorite store
to buy water and food.

Healthy food is the best option
because it will give me energy
and help me focus.

"Hello there, Mr. Hill.
I'm Tony, and I am here
to paint a wall, sir!"

"Okay, Tony.
These are the walls
I need painted today.
I know you will do
a great job!"

Before I paint,

I will need to prepare the room.

1. Cover any furniture with a dropcloth.
2. Cover the floor with a dropcloth.
3. Tape off any light switches or outlet covers where you will be painting.

I have to be careful!
The paint can is heavy and easy to spill.
I don't pour the paint while standing.
I crouch down, stir the paint,
and pour it into a paint tray.

Now I am ready
to paint the wall.
I always go up and down,
not side to side.

Before I clean up,
I will call Mr. Hill in
to inspect the work.
Mr. Hill approves
and has no changes.

I provide Mr. Hill with an invoice.

An **invoice** lists each item or service the customer was charged for.

INVOICE #0079

DATE: 3/14/2022

FROM:

NAME: Tony
COMPANY: Tony's Handyman Service
ADDRESS:
CITY, STATE:
ZIP, COUNTRY:
PHONE:
E-MAIL:
WEB:

TO:

NAME: Tyrone Hill
COMPANY:
ADDRESS:
CITY, STATE: Panama City, FL
ZIP, COUNTRY:
PHONE:
E-MAIL:
WEB:

FOR:

Num.	Goods, Services	Qty	Unit Price	Price
1	Paint two walls	1	$125	$125
2	Supplies	1	$25	$25
3				
4				
5				
6				
7				
8				
9				
	TOTAL:			$150

Mr. Hill is now ready to
pay me for my work.

He pays me,
and I provide him a receipt.

A receipt shows how much money
was received from the customer.

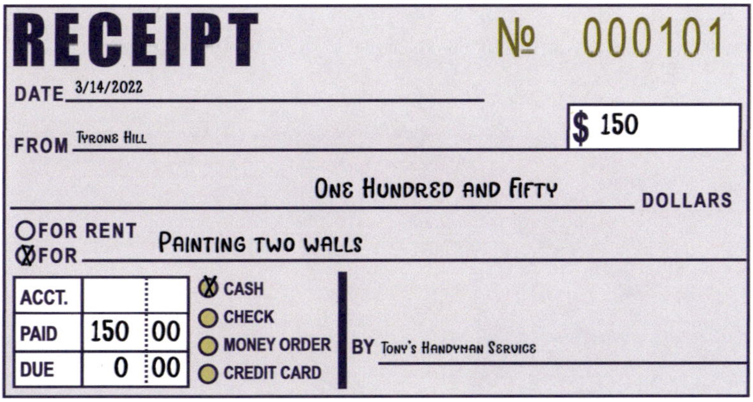
RECEIPT № 000101

DATE 3/14/2022

FROM Tyrone Hill $ 150

One Hundred and Fifty DOLLARS

○ FOR RENT
⊗ FOR Painting two walls

ACCT.		
PAID	150	00
DUE	0	00

⊗ CASH
○ CHECK
○ MONEY ORDER
○ CREDIT CARD

BY Tony's Handyman Service

Now it's time to clean
my tools and work area.
I also need to make it look nice.

I put my money in a special bank account that is just for saving money. It's called a savings account.

It's important to save my money so that I can invest it later. Investing money allows me to make more money.

Hello there! I'm Tony's wallet.
I help Tony add up his money.
Today Tony received
$150 for painting the wall
and a $50 bonus from Mr. Hill.

Tony made $200 today!

See you next time!
Remember to work safely,
collect your money, save it,
and invest it.

About the Illustrator

Benjamin Ogah

Benjamin Ogah is a traditional and digital illustrator that currently resides in Abuja, Nigeria.

He is a self-taught artist who specializes in a wide range of illustrations: comic books, character designs and, most recently, children books.

For inquiries, you can reach out to him via Linktree:

linktr.ee/thainhuman

About the Author

Tron Reynolds

Tron Reynolds is a business owner, musician, and author who lives in Panama City, Florida.

He has ten kids and one grandchild and somehow found time to write a book.

Connect with Tron:

facebook.com/tronreynolds
instagram.com/tronreynolds
reynoldsreadingbooks@gmail.com

Dedications

Antron Reynolds Jr.
Antwan Reynolds
Raquel Reynolds
Aniyah Reynolds
Amina Reynolds-Denson
Ranaya Reynolds
Antonio Reynolds
Anthony Reynolds
Asiah Reynolds
Ashton Reynolds
Aden Reynolds
Shakesha Reynolds
Trey Ross
Shica & Kids
Nikki & Kids
Sasha & Kids
Melinda Martin
Ohan Benjamin
Pamela Reynolds
Jean & Mark
Shawn & Elaine
Doreen Wallace

Carmela Jones
Jim & Gayle
Darrell Byrd
Morgan Weller
Janice & Gus
Jameson Christian
Henrietta
Jon Miller
Robert Thaxton
Thomas Pituch
Yobe Qiu
Ron B.
James Bennett
Lucille Reynolds
Darlene & Oscar
Reynolds PropServ, LLC
Reynolds Auto Detailing
Reynolds Southern Deli
Reynolds Reading Books
D. Reynolds
K. Ross
P. Edwards

CERTIFICATE

OF COMPLETION

This Certificate Is Proudly Presented To

____

Made in the USA
Monee, IL
05 November 2026

67375729R00019